Copyright © 2008 by Quirk Productions, Inc.

All rights reserved. No part of this book may be reproduced in
any form without written permission from the publisher.

Library of Congress Cataloging in Publication Number: 2007939943

ISBN: 978-1-59474-229-3

Printed in China
Typeset in Bad Neighborhood, Frankie, Helvetica Neue, Imperfect

Designed by Bryn Ashburn

Distributed in North America by Chronicle Books
680 Second Street
San Francisco, CA 94107

10 9 8 7 6 5 4 3 2

Quirk Books
215 Church Street
Philadelphia, PA 19106
www.quirkbooks.com

Photo Credits

Library of Congress, Yanker Poster Collection: 15, 74 & 77 (Courtesy Chris Gorman), 128, 138, 164; Images
© Stockphoto.com: 27, 36, 40, 44–45, 49, 54–55, 82–83, 85, 86–87, 88, 94–95, 98–99, 118–19, 153, 158,
169, 175; AP Images: 28–29, 41, 102–3, 127, 144–45, 154–55, 170, 172–73; Propaganda © 2007 by
Micah Ian Wright and www.AntiWarPosters.com: 22–23, 52, 106; *Journée Nationale de la Paix*, by Jean
Carlu, Musée des Deux Guerres Mondiales, Paris/Bridgeman Art Library/Archives Charmet © Artists Rights
Society (ARS), New York / ADAGP, Paris: 16; George Chartier © Fabrica, 2001, from the project "Visions of
Change 9/11" (www.anti-war.us): 19; *Never Again*, Musée d'Histoire Contemporaine, B.D.I.C., Paris/Bridgeman
Art Library/Archives Charmet: 33; Propaganda poster of the French communist party, Private
Collection/Bridgeman Art Library: 39; Photo courtesy Christopher Rainone (www.monkeylens.com): 50–51;
Anti-Vietnam war poster satirizing Richard Nixon, Private Collection/Bridgeman Art Library/Peter Newark
American Pictures: 58; *What Do YOU Say AMERICA?* National Archives Trust, Pennsylvania, USA/Bridgeman Art
Library: 61; *I Want You for U.S. Army*, 1972, Smithsonian Institution, Washington D.C., USA/Bridgeman Art
Library/Held Collection: 65; *United for the Liberation*, Musée des Deux Guerres Mondiales, Paris/Bridgeman Art
Library/Archives Charmet: 66; *Justice!* Second World War poster, Private Collection/Bridgeman Art
Library/Giraudon: 70; Courtesy NASA: 92–93; *Skull (War Is Not the Answer)*, 2003, Courtesy Brandon Bauer
(www.anti-war.us): 115; *What About Me? Labour for Peace*, Musée des Deux Guerres Mondiales,
Paris/Bridgeman Art Library/Archives Charmet: 124; *Women of Britain, Come into the Factories*, Stapleton
Collection, UK/Bridgeman Art Library: 133; *The Dove That Goes Bang!* Private Collection/Bridgeman Art
Library/Archives Charmet: 148–49.

The
ANTI-WAR
QUOTE BOOK

EDITED BY ERIC GROVES, SR.

QUIRK BOOKS
PHILADELPHIA

THERE NEVER
WAS A GOOD WAR OR
A BAD PEACE.

Benjamin Franklin
(1706–1790), American statesman, writer, and inventor

introduction

We cannot afford any more war.

The costs are too enormous. History's greatest philosophers, educators, politicians, scientists, artists, clergy, and soldiers have argued this point for more than four thousand years.

Will we listen?

The Anti-War Quote Book contains the collected wisdom of men and women from diverse cultures and eras, all preaching against war. Unless humanity embraces their message of peace and renounces its insane lust for war, then, as physicist Dr. Carl Sagan warned in his 1983 book *The Nuclear Winter*: "There seems to be a real possibility of the extinction of the human species." If you're unconvinced that warfare can end humanity, read further in *The Nuclear Winter*: "The World Health Organization, in a recent detailed study . . . concludes that 1.1 billion people would be killed outright in . . . a nuclear war, mainly in the United States, the Soviet Union, Europe, China and Japan. An additional 1.1 billion people would suffer serious . . . radiation sickness, for which medical help would be unavailable. It thus seems possible that more than 2 billion people—almost half of all the humans on Earth—would be destroyed in the immediate aftermath of a global thermonuclear war."

Yet Dr. Sagan meant nuclear holocaust. Many people no longer perceive nuclear war as a threat, especially since the collapse of the Soviet Union in the late 1980s.

They should think again.

On April 4, 2005, thirty-two Nobel laureates signed a resolution drafted by the

Association of World Citizens that states: "We call on the governments of the United States, Russia, China, France, and the U.K., India, Pakistan, Israel, and North Korea to support and implement steps to lower the operational status of nuclear weapons systems in order to reduce the risk of nuclear catastrophe and . . . achieve the elimination of nuclear weapons under strict and effective international control. We note that . . . thousands of nuclear weapons in the U.S. and Russia are on launch-on-warning status, and that the megatonnage involved remains more than enough to destroy civilization and perhaps the human race."

Even if you set aside the traditional threat from Russia, many other countries stand ready to acquire, and use, nuclear weapons. In *Nuclear Terrorism* (2004), Professor Graham Allison of Harvard University describes a meeting in 2001 between al Qaeda leader Osama bin Laden—architect of the 9/11 attacks on American soil—and Sultan Mahmood and Abdul Majeed, two officials of Pakistan's nuclear weapons program. Allison writes, "Pakistani officials indicated that Mahmood and Majeed 'spoke extensively about weapons of mass destruction,' and provided detailed responses to bin Laden's questions about the manufacture of nuclear . . . weapons." In a 1998 pamphlet titled *The Nuclear Bomb of Islam*, bin Laden made clear that "it is the duty of Muslims to prepare as much force as possible to terrorize the enemies of God."

What if bin Laden's followers acquire a nuclear weapon? Allison notes that a small ten-kiloton bomb could be smuggled by car into New York City. If it were detonated in Times Square, one million people would die instantly. The resulting fire, radiation, and aftereffects would cause thousands of additional casualties.

Then there are chemical weapons. In 1995, the fanatical Aum Shinrikyo religious cult released toxic sarin nerve gas into the Tokyo subway system, killing twelve and injuring more than five thousand. Cult members believe in a global doomsday and have tried to hasten the apocalypse through chemical-weapons attacks. Author Kyle B. Olson, in a 1999 online article for the Centers for Disease Control and Prevention, warns, "[Aum Shinrikyo's leader, Shoko Ashahara] has frequently preached about a coming Armageddon, which he describes as a global conflict." Still, if you choose not to believe in the doomsday scenarios of nuclear or chemical attacks, at least consider the more familiar horrors of the endless conventional wars raging worldwide.

In Uganda, Africa, the civil war between President Yoweri Museveni's troops and the insurgent Lord's Resistance Army (LRA), led by Joseph Kony, has lasted nineteen years, resulting in horrific killings that continue today. Some one hundred thousand Ugandans died during the conflict, and 1.5 million refugees still live in huge Internally Displaced Persons (IDP) camps. During the conflict, LRA rebels kidnapped 25,000 young boys and turned them into child soldiers, most of whom were either killed in combat or dumped into temporary shelters called reception houses. All the boys were horribly mutilated.

In Congo (formerly Zaire), Africa, fighting continues among armed bands from the Second Congo War—a conflict that supposedly ended in 2002 but still claims lives. The war encompassed nine African nations and killed almost four million people. The slaughter continues.

At the time this book went to press in November 2007, the US-Iraq War had claimed the lives of 3,815 U.S. soldiers and wounded 27,753 more. The body counts increase daily. In addition, 1,304 allied troops and other "contractors" (mercenaries) have been killed, with nearly 10,825 wounded. The Iraqi military forces of Saddam Hussein sustained losses in excess of 30,000 troops, according to a statement issued by U.S. General Tommy Franks following the initial 2003 invasion; the present coalition-trained Iraqi Security Forces have lost approximately 7,479. Iraqi civilians, the worst-hit group, have suffered an astounding 645,965 deaths to date, an average of 2.5 percent of Iraq's pre-war population. Current overall death totals: 696,560 men, women, and children. These numbers seem destined to rise, for no political or military end to the conflict is in sight.

We can't afford any more wars.

Listen to General of the Army Douglas MacArthur, who served as the Supreme Allied Commander during World War II and who remains the most decorated soldier in U.S. history. Standing on the decks of the battleship *Missouri* in 1945, he urged the need to end all wars: "Men since the beginning of time have sought peace. Various methods through the ages have attempted to devise an international process to prevent or settle disputes between nations. . . . Military alliance, balances of power, leagues of nations all in turn failed, leaving the only path to be the way of the crucible of war. The utter destructiveness of war now blots out this alternative. We have had our last chance. If we do not now devise some greater and more equitable system,

Armageddon will be at our door. The problem basically is theological and involves a spiritual recrudescence and improvement of human character that will synchronize with our almost matchless advances in science, art, literature, and all material and cultural developments of the past two thousand years. It must be of the spirit if we are to save the flesh."

Similarly, General of the Army Dwight D. Eisenhower, the Supreme Commander of the victorious Allied forces in Europe during World War II, also spoke of the need to end war. In a 1956 letter to his friend Richard Leo Simon, a New York publisher, he wrote: "When we get to the point, as some day we will, that both sides know that in any outbreak of general hostilities, regardless of the element of surprise, destruction will be both reciprocal and complete, possibly we will have sense enough to meet at the conference table with the understanding that the era of armaments has ended and the human race must conform its actions to this truth or die."

I hope *The Anti-War Quote Book* will renew your faith that one day we will wipe the scourge of war from the Earth. In the words of the biblical prophet Isaiah (2:4): "And he shall judge among the nations . . . and they shall beat their swords into plowshares, and their spears into pruninghooks: nation shall not lift up sword against nation, neither shall they learn war any more."

When war begins, then hell openeth.

George Herbert
(1593–1633), Welsh poet and priest

Never, never, never believe any war will
be smooth and easy, or that anyone who embarks
on the strange voyage can measure the tides
and hurricanes he will encounter. The statesman
who yields to war fever must realize that once
the signal is given, he is no longer the master
of policy but the slave of unforeseeable
and uncontrollable events.

Winston Churchill
(1874–1965), British politician and Nobel laureate

All wars are popular for the first thirty days.

Arthur Schlesinger Jr.
(1917–2007), American historian and social critic

WAR IS CRUELTY, AND YOU CANNOT REFINE IT.

William Tecumseh Sherman
(1820–1891), American Civil War general

✿

WAR IS A BANKRUPTCY OF POLICY.

Hans Von Seeckt
(1866–1936), German military officer

✿

WAR IS NOT HEALTHY FOR CHILDREN AND OTHER LIVING THINGS.

Lorraine Schneider
(1925–1972), American artist and activist

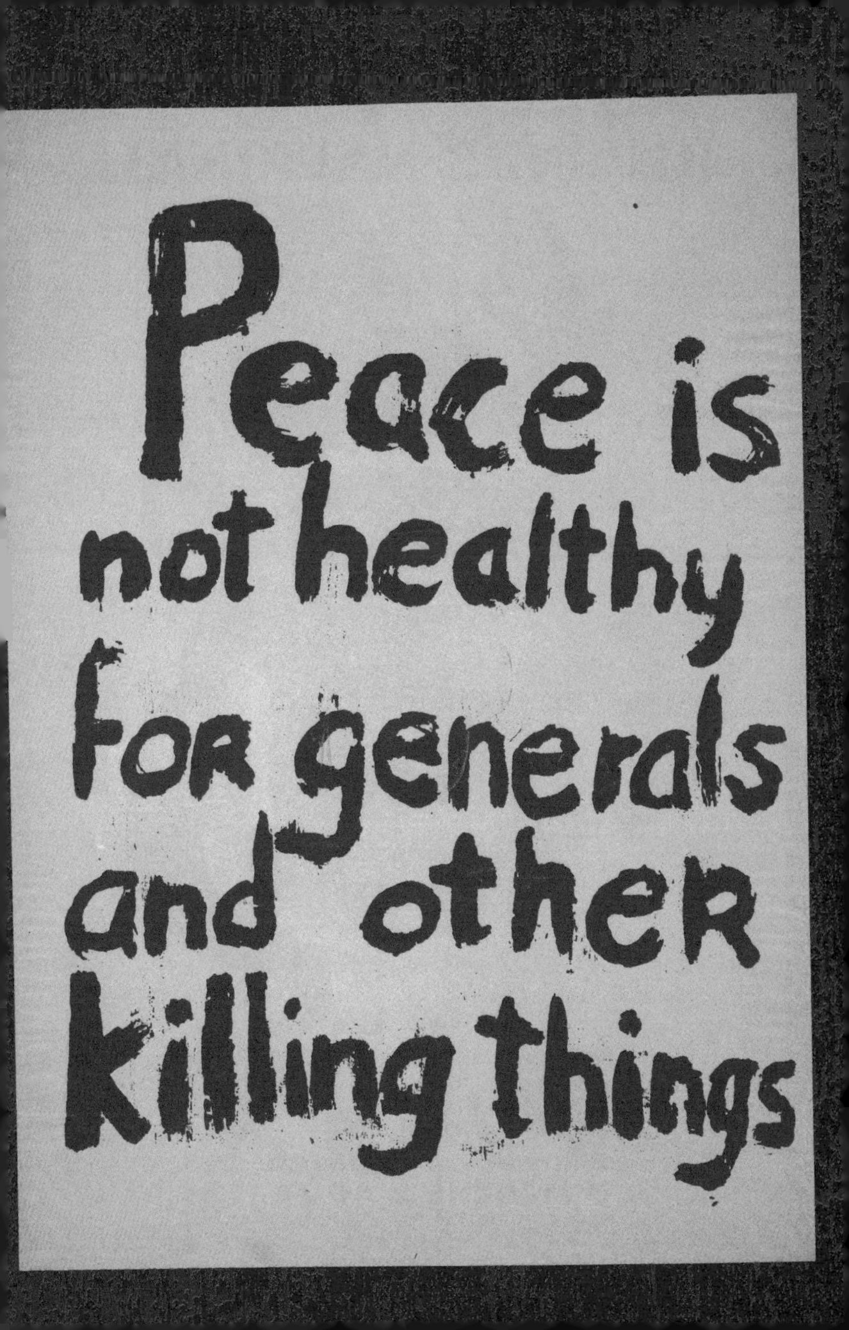
Peace is
not healthy
for generals
and other
killing things

Everything in war is barbaric. . . . But the worst barbarity of war is that it forces men collectively to commit acts which individually they would revolt with their whole being.

Ellen Key
(1849–1926), Swedish feminist writer

I do not recollect in all the animal kingdom a single species but man which is eternally and systematically engaged in the destruction of its own species.

Thomas Jefferson
(1743–1826), American president

My first wish is to see this plague to mankind banished from off the Earth, and the sons and daughters of this world employed in more pleasing and innocent amusements than in preparing implements and exercising them for the destruction of mankind.

George Washington
(1732–1799), American president

Though it seems that, among the people of the world, relatively few want or enjoy wars, and very many suffer in many ways during wars, man persists in this senseless behavior century after century.

George Brock Chisholm
(1896–1971), first director-general of the World Health Organization

A great war leaves a country with three armies: an army of cripples, an army of mourners, and an army of thieves.

Anonymous German saying

One is left with the horrible feeling now that war settles nothing; that to win a war is as disastrous as to lose one.

Agatha Christie
(1890–1976), English novelist

O Lord our Father, our young patriots, idols of our hearts, go forth to battle—be Thou near them! With them, in spirit, we also go forth from the sweet peace of our beloved firesides to smite the foe. O Lord our God, help us to tear their soldiers to bloody shreds with our shells; help us to cover their smiling fields with the pale forms of their patriot dead; help us to drown the thunder of the guns with the shrieks of their wounded writhing in pain; help us to lay waste their humble homes with a hurricane of fire; help us to wring the hearts of their unoffending widows with unavailing grief; help us to turn them out roofless with their little children to wander unfriended the wastes of their desolated land in rags and hunger and thirst, sports of the sun flames of summer and the icy winds of winter, broken in spirit, worn with travail, imploring Thee for the refuge of the grave and denied it—for our sakes who adore Thee, Lord, blast their hopes, blight their lives, protract their bitter pilgrimage, make heavy their steps, water their way with their tears, stain the white snow with the blood of their wounded feet! We ask it, in the spirit of love, of Him Who is the Source of Love, and Who is the ever—faithful refuge and friend of all that are sore beset and seek His aid with humble and contrite hearts. Amen.

Mark Twain
(1835–1910), American writer

In war, as it is waged now, with the enormous losses on both sides, both sides will lose. It is a form of mutual suicide; and I believe that the entire effort of modern society should be concentrated on an endeavor to outlaw war as a method of the solution of problems between nations.

Douglas MacArthur

(1880–1964), American army general

Today, the world is so small and so inter-dependent that the concept of war has become anachronistic, an outmoded approach.

Tenzin Gyatso

(1935–), fourteenth Dalai Lama

WIRELESS
Push-Buttons Make

A MESSAGE

PRINTED FOR H M STATIONERY OFFICE BY HAYCOCK PRESS, LONDON. S - RQ/O

WAR
ling So Much Easier

THE MINISTRY OF HOMELAND SECURITY

Pat Keely 43

EITHER MAN IS OBSOLETE, OR WAR IS.

Richard Buckminster Fuller
(1895–1983), American author and inventor

THANK GOD, MEN CANNOT AS YET FLY, AND LAY WASTE THE SKY AS WELL AS THE EARTH!

Henry David Thoreau
(1817–1862), American author and philosopher

WE MUST CONQUER WAR, OR WAR WILL CONQUER US.

Ely Culbertson
(1891–1955), American activist

history

History is a bath of blood.

William James
(1842–1910), American
psychologist and philosopher

I have noticed that, as soon as you have soldiers, the story is called history. Before their arrival it is called myth, folktale, legend, fairy tale, oral poetry, ethnography. After the soldiers arrive, it is called history.

Paula Gunn • (1939–), American poet and activist

War makes rattling good history; but peace is poor reading.

Thomas Hardy • (1840–1928), British novelist and poet

History is a vast early-warning system.

Norman Cousins • (1915–1990), American author and activist

Throughout history, the world has been laid waste to ensure the triumph of conceptions that are now as dead as the men that died for them.

Henri de Montherlant • (1896–1972), French essayist and novelist

AFTER EACH WAR THERE IS A LITTLE LESS DEMOCRACY TO SAVE.

Brooks Atkinson
(1894–1984), American journalist

You can't say civilizations don't advance . . .
for in every war they kill you in a new way.

Will Rogers
(1879–1935), American humorist and social commentator

It is horrible to see everything that one
detested in the past coming back wearing
the colors of the future.

Jean Rostand
(1894–1977), French philosopher and biologist

THOSE WHO CANNOT REMEMBER THE PAST ARE CONDEMNED TO REPEAT IT.

George Santayana
(1863–1952), Spanish-born philosopher and writer

INTERNÉS ET DÉPORTÉS POLITIQUES
FAMILLES DES INTERNÉS ET DÉPORTÉS POLITIQUES

contre les hommes et les instruments de la trahison
pour la défense de vos intérêts matériels et moraux
pour sauver de l'oubli votre martyre et en faire une arme
pour que nous mêmes et nos enfants ne revoyions...

plus jamais ça !

TOUS UNIS pour la renaissance de notre patrie
pour une paix féconde par l'union de tous les alliés

Adhérez à la
FÉDÉRATION NATIONALE des DÉPORTÉS et INTERNÉS PATRIOTES
10, RUE LEROUX, PARIS 16ᵉ

empires

The responsibility of the
great states is to serve, and not
to dominate, the world.

Harry S. Truman
(1884–1972), American president

Of all tyrannies, a tyranny
exercised "for the good of
its victims" may be the
most oppressive.

C. S. Lewis
(1898–1963), Irish author and scholar

THIS AND NO OTHER IS THE ROOT FROM WHICH A TYRANT SPRINGS: WHEN HE FIRST APPEARS, HE IS A PROTECTOR.

Plato
(427–347 BC),
Greek philosopher

The United States of America is still run by its citizens. The government works for us. Rank imperialism and warmongering are not American traditions or values. We do not need to dominate the world. We want and need to work with other nations. We want to find solutions other than killing people.

Molly Ivins
(1944–2007), American author and political commentator

History is replete with examples of empires mounting impressive military campaigns on the cusp of their impending economic collapse.

Eric Alterman
(1960–), American journalist

The first accounts we have of mankind are but accounts of their butcheries. All empires have been cemented in blood.

Edmund Burke
(1729–1797), Irish statesman and political theorist

The conquest of the earth, which mostly means the taking it away from those who have a different complexion or slightly flatter noses than ourselves, is not a pretty thing when you look into it.

Joseph Chamberlain
(1836–1914), British politician

Imperialism, like dictatorship, sears the soul, degrades the spirit, and makes individuals small, the better to rule them. Fear and cowardice are its allies. Imperialism is government of other people, by other people, and for other people.

Louis Fischer
(1896–1970), Jewish American journalist

The economic root of imperialism is the desire of strong organized industrial and financial interests to secure and develop, at the public expense and by the public force, markets for their surplus goods and their surplus capital. War, militarism and a "spirited foreign policy" are the necessary means to this end.

John Atkinson Hobson
(1858–1940), English economist

NON !
LA FRANCE NE SERA PAS
UN PAYS COLONISÉ !

LES AMÉRICAINS ᴇɴ AMÉRIQUE !

ÉDITÉ PAR LE PARTI COMMUNISTE FRANÇAIS

IF THERE BE ONE PRINCIPLE MORE DEEPLY ROOTED THAN ANY OTHER IN THE MIND OF EVERY AMERICAN, IT IS THAT WE SHOULD HAVE NOTHING TO DO WITH CONQUEST.

Thomas Jefferson
(1743–1826), American president

power

What is needed is a realization that power without love is reckless and abusive and that love without power is sentimental and anemic. Power at its best is love implementing the demands of justice.

Martin Luther King Jr.

(1929–1968), American civil rights leader and Nobel laureate

The vaster the power gained, the vaster the appetite for more.

Ursula K. Le Guin

(1929–), American author

A strong nation, like a strong person, can afford to be gentle, firm, thoughtful, and restrained. It can afford to extend a helping hand to others. It's a weak nation, like a weak person, that must behave with bluster and boasting and rashness and other signs of insecurity.

Jimmy Carter

(1924–), American president and Nobel laureate

It is not power that corrupts, but fear.
The fear of losing power corrupts those who wield it,
and fear of scourge of power corrupts those
who are subject to it.

Aung San Suu Kyi • (1945–), Burmese activist

All ferocity is born from weakness.

Lucius Annaeus Seneca the Younger
(ca. 4 BC–AD 65), Roman philosopher

DO YOU KNOW . . . WHAT AMAZES ME IN THE
WORLD? THE INABILITY OF FORCE TO MAIN-
TAIN ANYTHING AT ALL. THERE ARE ONLY
TWO POWERS IN THE WORLD: THE SWORD
AND THE MIND. IN THE LONG RUN, THE
SWORD IS ALWAYS DEFEATED BY THE MIND.

Napoleon Bonaparte
(1769–1821), French emperor

DO NOT EVER SAY THAT THE DESIRE TO "DO GOOD" BY FORCE IS A GOOD MOTIVE. NEITHER POWER-LUST NOR STUPIDITY ARE GOOD MOTIVES.

Ayn Rand
(1905–1982), Russian-born American novelist and philosopher

money

ENDLESS MONEY FORMS THE SINEWS OF WAR.

Cicero
(106–43 BC), Roman statesman and philosopher

War seldom enters
but where wealth allures.
John Dryden
(1631–1700), English writer and literary critic

NOT M

Make wars **unprofitable**
and you make them **impossible.**

A. Philip Randolph • (1889–1979), African
American civil rights leader

We're on our Way!

We Want That Oil!

Stick to your Job—Oil is Ammunition

A MESSAGE FROM THE MINISTRY OF HOMELAND SECURITY

Presently, we have so many wars at the local, national, and international levels because we have invested in the commodities of war. Not everyone wants peace; some people benefit economically from instability, insecurity, and warfare. Until we dismantle that and get to the root causes of why we have violent conflicts, we will not achieve peace.

Noeleen Heyzer
(1948–), Singaporean executive director of
the United Nations Development Fund for Women (UNIFEM)

It's our taxes that are paying for the wars in Afghanistan and Colombia. Bombs are being dropped that kill innocent people. And our money is paying for those bombs. We have to take responsibility. We have to say: This is our money. The check that I sent the IRS is being used to make bombs. And today, with the tightening U.S. budget, we're being asked for more money than ever before to make more bombs. We can look at it from a very personal viewpoint. When they talk about war, we're the ones who end up paying for it.

Dolores Huerta
(1930–), cofounder of United Farm Workers of America

The master class has always declared the wars; the subject class has always fought the battles. The master class has had all to gain and nothing to lose, while the subject class has had nothing to gain and all to lose—especially their lives.

Eugene Victor Debs
(1855–1926), American labor and political leader

The church allows people to believe that they can be good Christians and yet draw dividends from armament factories, can be good Christians and yet imperil the well-being of their fellows by speculating in stocks and shares, can be good Christians and yet be imperialists, yet participate in war.

Aldous Leonard Huxley
(1894–1963), English author

Of course it is tempting to close one's eyes to history and instead to speculate about the roots of war in some possible animal instinct: as if, like a tiger, we still had to kill to live, or, like the robin redbreast, to defend a nesting territory. But war, organized war, is not a human instinct. It is a highly planned and cooperative form of theft. And that form of theft began ten thousand years ago when the harvesters of wheat accumulated a surplus and the nomads rose out of the desert to rob them of what they themselves could not provide.

Jacob Bronowski

(1908–1974), Polish-born British mathematician

leader-
ship

There is a demand today for men who can make wrong appear right.

Terence
(ca. 190–159 BC), Roman playwright

The cry has been that when war is declared, all opposition should therefore be hushed. A sentiment more unworthy of a free country could hardly be propagated. If the doctrine be admitted, rulers have only to declare war, and they are screened at once from scrutiny.

William Ellery Channing
(1780–1842), American theologian

Name me an emperor who was ever struck by a cannonball.

Charles V
(1500–1558), Holy Roman Emperor

Would you buy a used WAR from this man?

STRIKE! NOV 14
MARCH ON WASHINGTON
& SAN FRANCISCO NOV 15

BRING ALL THE GIS HOME NOW!

STUDENT MOBILIZATION COMMITTEE TO END THE WAR IN VIETNAM, 1029 VERMONT AVE NW, WASHINGTON DC, 20005, 202—737— 0072

Blind faith in your leaders or
in anything will get you killed.

Bruce Springsteen

(1949–) American singer-songwriter

Fuehrers will cease to plague the world
only when the majority of its inhabitants
regard such adventurers with the same
disgust as they now bestow on swindlers and
pimps. So long as men worship the Caesars
and Napoleons, Caesars and Napoleons will
duly rise and make them miserable.

Aldous Leonard Huxley

(1894–1963), English author

My theory is, strong people
don't need strong leaders.

Ella Baker

(1903–1986), African American civil rights worker

WHEN THE TYRANT HAS DISPOSED OF FOREIGN ENEMIES BY CONQUEST OR TREATY, AND THERE IS NOTHING TO FEAR FROM THEM, THEN HE IS ALWAYS STIRRING UP SOME WAR OR OTHER, IN ORDER THAT THE PEOPLE MAY REQUIRE A LEADER.

Plato

(427–347 BC), Greek philosopher

"We consider peace a catastrophe for human civilization"

— *MUSSOLINI*

What do YOU say, AMERICA?

Issued by the Graphics Division, Office of War Information, Washington, D.C.

propa-
ganda

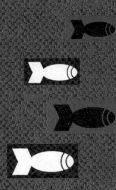

The first casualty,
when war comes,
is truth.

Hiram Johnson
(1866–1945), U.S. senator

Almost all propaganda is designed to create fear. Heads of governments and their officials know that a frightened people is easier to govern, will forfeit rights it would otherwise defend, is less likely to demand a better life, and will agree to millions and millions being spent on "Defense."

John Boynton Priestly
(1894–1984), English writer

They have always taught and trained you to believe it to be your patriotic duty to go to war and to have yourselves slaughtered at their command. But in all the history of the world, you, the people, have never had a voice in declaring war, and strange as it certainly appears, no war by any nation in any age has ever been declared by the people.

Eugene Victor Debs
(1855–1926), American labor and political leader

Old men declare wars because they have failed to solve complex political and economic problems. They then send young men to go fight them. Of course, the old men have to make up patriotic and emotional rationales to justify their stupidity.

Arthur Hoppe
(1925–2000), American writer

I WANT YOU
FOR U.S. ARMY
NEAREST RECRUITING STATION

UNIS POUR LA
LIBERATION

Propaganda is the art of persuading others what you don't believe yourself.

Abba Eban

(1915–2002), Israeli diplomat and politician

Propaganda, as inverted patriotism, draws nourishment from the sins of the enemy. If there are no sins, invent them! The aim is to make the enemy appear so great a monster that he forfeits the rights of a human being.

Ian Hamilton

(1853–1947), British general

"Terrorism" is what we call the violence of the weak, and we condemn it; "war" is what we call the violence of the strong, and we glorify it.

Sydney J. Harris

(1917–1986), American journalist and columnist

WAR IS AT BEST BARBARISM... ITS GLORY IS ALL MOONSHINE IT IS ONLY THOSE WHO HAVE NEITHER FIRED A SHOT NOR HEARD THE SHRIEKS AND GROANS OF THE WOUNDED, WHO CRY ALOUD FOR BLOOD, MORE VENGEANCE, MORE DESOLATION WAR IS HELL.

William Tecumseh Sherman • (1820–1891), American Civil War general

They wrote in the old days that it is sweet and fitting to die for one's country. But in modern war there is nothing sweet nor fitting in your dying. You will die like a dog for no good reason.

Ernest Hemingway
(1899–1961), American writer and Nobel laureate

Literature has invented a fiction which still inspires boys and old men and romanticists. Vague remembrances of Marathon and Thermopylae blend with medieval tales of chivalry. Pictures of hand-to-hand conflict according to the rules, of chivalrous reconciliations, of mutual honor and respect, move confusedly before the imagination. The sentiment and ethic of a method of war as extinct as the Stone Age are applied to what has long ago become a matter of cold-blooded calculation and organized butchery by machines.

Goldsworthy Lowes Dickinson
(1862–1932), English historian and political activist

If peace . . . only had the music and pageantry of war, there'd be no wars.

Sophie Kerr
(1880–1965), American writer

JUSTICE!

W.Z.

When war

enters a country

it

produces

lies

like

sand.

Arthur Ponsonby
(1871–1946), British politician,
writer, and social activist

enemies

FRIENDS MAY COME AND GO, BUT ENEMIES ACCUMULATE.

Thomas Hudson Jones
(1892–1969), American sculptor

RALLY TO PROTEST BRITISH TERRORISM IN NORTHERN IRELAND
ED KOCH / WILLIAM F. RYAN / PETE FITZPATRICK / LIAM KELLY /
FINBAR O'KANE / MĀIRE BRADSHAW / JOAN McKIERNAN / SEAN
KENNY / ENTERTAINMENT / SPONSOR—SAOR EIRE CUMANN
SATURDAY JUNE 3RD—12:00 NOON / 85TH ST. AND 3RD AVE.

THE FACE OF THE ENEMY FRIGHTENS ME ONLY WHEN I SEE HOW MUCH IT RESEMBLES MINE.

Stanislaw J. Lec

(1909–1966), Polish writer

WE HAVE GOT TO UNDERSTAND THAT THEY DREAM OUR DREAMS AND WE DREAM THEIRS. WE HAVE GOT TO UNDERSTAND THAT THEY ARE US.

Rachel Corrie

(1979–2003), American peace activist

We make "national honor" God; and we fail
to see the presence of God in other cultures and
traditions and people. We make human color
and gender the color and gender of God; and we
fail to see God in the one who comes in different
shades and other forms than ours, though all of
our scriptures are clear about equality and all
those theologies are sound. . . . We're all
simply in it together, swimming together in
the energy that is God. All of us.

Sister Joan D. Chittister
(1936–), Benedictine nun

The more I think about peace, I think peace
starts and ends in connection. When we connect,
we learn about "the other." It's not tolerance
but understanding, acceptance. In the
connection, everything starts to happen.

Isabel Allende
(1942–), Chilean American author

W Chris Gorman Associates

If we could read the secret history of our enemies, we should find in each man's life sorrow and suffering enough to disarm all hostility.

Henry Wadsworth Longfellow

(1807–1882), American poet

✿

The chain of animosity cannot be broken by retaliating against your enemy. Human beings are foolish. How many times are the same mistakes repeated?

Jakucho Setouchi

(1922–), Japanese Buddhist nun

✿

When old enemies disappear, mellow, or turn into allies, as frequently happens in international relations, new enemies must be found and new threats must be discovered. The failure to replenish the supply of enemies is the supreme threat facing any national security bureaucracy.

Richard Barnet

(1929–2004), American scholar and activist

OUR ENEMIES' OPINION OF US
COMES CLOSER TO THE TRUTH
THAN OUR OWN.

François La Rochefoucauld
(1613–1680), French writer

WHO IS A HERO? HE
WHO TURNS HIS ENEMY
INTO A FRIEND.

The Talmud

violence

IF IT'S NATURAL TO
KILL, WHY DO MEN HAVE
TO GO INTO TRAINING
TO LEARN WAR?

Joan Baez
(1941–), folk singer and activist

VIOLENCE IS AN
ADMISSION THAT ONE'S
IDEAS AND GOALS
CANNOT PREVAIL ON
THEIR OWN MERITS.

Edward M. Kennedy
(1932–), American senator

VIOLENCE IS
THE LAST REFUGE OF
THE INCOMPETENT.

Isaac Asimov
(1920–1992), Russian-born American author

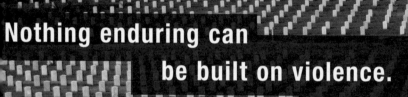

Nothing enduring can be built on violence.

Mahatma Gandhi
(1869–1948), Indian spiritual and political leader

The practice of violence, like all action, changes the world,
but the most probable change is to a more violent world.

Hannah Arendt • (1906–1975), German Jewish political theorist

The graveyards are full of indispensable men.

Charles de Gaulle
(1890–1970), French military leader and statesman

Violence as a way of achieving racial justice
is both impractical and immoral. It is impractical
because it is a descending spiral ending in
destruction for all. The old law of an eye for
an eye leaves everybody blind.

Martin Luther King Jr.
(1929–1968), American civil rights leader and Nobel laureate

Violence and injury enclose in their net
all that do such things and generally return
upon him who began.

Lucretius
(99–55 BC), Roman poet and philosopher

Pray for the welfare of the government,
for were it not for the fear of the government,
a man would swallow up his neighbors alive.

The Talmud

No body of men can be induced to do another man's killing for him unless he can convince them that they may honorably do so. The percentage of blackguards and sadists who enjoy cruelty for its own sake have to pretend that they are patriots and ministers of justice to secure the toleration of their fellow citizens.

George Bernard Shaw
(1856–1950), Irish dramatist and political activist

It is forbidden to kill; therefore all murderers are punished unless they kill in large numbers and to the sound of trumpets.

Voltaire
(François-Marie Arouet; 1694–1778), French writer and philosopher

The world is drenched in mutual slaughter. . . . Held to be a crime when committed by individuals, homicide is called a virtue when committed by the state.

Saint Cyprian
(3rd century), Carthaginian bishop and early Christian writer

Kill a man, and you are an assassin.
Kill millions of men, and you are a conqueror.
Kill everyone, and you are a god.

Jean Rostand
(1894–1977), French philosopher and biologist

The one who thinks that the Spirit is a slayer, and the one who thinks the Spirit is slain, both are ignorant. Because the Spirit neither slays nor is slain.

Bhagavad Gita

He who, seeking his own happiness, punishes or kills beings, who also longs for happiness, will not find happiness after death.

Buddha
(Siddhartha Gautama; ca. 563–483 BC),
Indian spiritual teacher

THE **DEAD** KNOW ONLY ONE THING: IT IS **BETTER** TO BE **ALIVE**

Elroy James Flecker
(1884–1915), English poet and novelist

Do not men die fast enough without being
destroyed by each other?

François Fénelon
(1651–1715), French Roman-Catholic theologian

The least pain in our little finger gives more
concern and uneasiness than the destruction
of millions of our fellow beings.

William Hazlitt
(1778–1830), English writer

So long as governments set the example
of killing their enemies, private individuals
will occasionally kill theirs.

Elbert Hubbard
(1856–1915), American writer, artist, and philosopher

nukes

Human history becomes more and more a race between education and catastrophe.

H. G. Wells
(1866–1946), English writer

If the Third World War is fought with nuclear weapons, the fourth will be fought with bows and arrows.

Louis Mountbatten
(1900–1979), British admiral and statesman

The release of atomic energy has not created a new problem. It has merely made more urgent the necessity of solving an existing one.

Albert Einstein
(1879–1955), German-born physicist and Nobel laureate

It has become almost banal to say that the atomic age has fundamentally altered the nature of war. No nuclear power can tell another: "Do as I say or I shall kill you" but is reduced to saying: "Do as I say or I shall kill us both," which is an entirely different matter.

John G. Stoessinger
(1927–), American political analyst and author

Today every inhabitant of this planet must contemplate the day when this planet may no longer be habitable. Every man, woman, and child lives under a nuclear sword of Damocles, hanging by the slenderest of threads, capable of being cut at any moment by accident or miscalculation or madness.

John F. Kennedy
(1917–1963), American president

THERE IS NO EVIL IN THE ATOM, ONLY IN MEN'S SOULS.

Adlai Stevenson
(1900–1965), American politician

Weapons are like money; no one knows
the meaning of *enough*.

Martin Amis • (1949–), English novelist

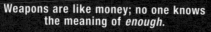

Every gun that is made, every warship
launched, every rocket fired, signifies in
a final sense a theft from those who
hunger and are not fed—those who are
cold and are not clothed. This world in
arms is not spending its money alone—
it is spending the sweat of its laborers,
the genius of its scientists, the hopes
of its children.

Dwight D. Eisenhower • (1890–1969), American president

It is hard for me to understand a culture
that spends more on wars and weapons
to kill than it does on education and
welfare to help and develop.

Dan George • (1899–1981), Canadian actor and chief
of the Tsleil-Waututh people

CATION AND

JOBS

WAR

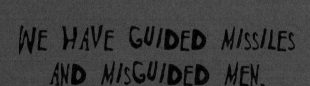

WE HAVE GUIDED MISSILES
AND MISGUIDED MEN.

Martin Luther King Jr.
(1929–1968), American civil rights leader and Nobel laureate

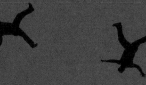

Hiroshima signaled a failure of mankind, not just of the United States. The growth of technology has far outstripped our ability to use it wisely. Like a quarrelling group of monkeys on a leaky boat, armed with sticks of dynamite, we are embarked on an uncertain journey.

Pervez Hoodbhoy
(1950–), Pakistani professor of nuclear physics

As the [first atomic] bomb fell over Hiroshima and exploded, we saw an entire city disappear. I wrote in my log the words: "My God, what have we done?"

Robert Lewis
(1909–1997), American actor, director, and educator

I believe that there is a greater power in the world than the evil power of military force, of nuclear bombs—there is the power of good, of morality, of humanitarianism.

Linus Carl Pauling
(1901–1994), American chemist

I appeal as a human being to human beings: Remember your humanity and forget the rest. If you can do so, the way lies open to a new Paradise; if you cannot, nothing lies before you but universal death.

Bertrand Russell
(1872–1970), Welsh philosopher and activist

Except for fools and madmen, everyone knows that nuclear war would be an unprecedented human catastrophe. A more or less typical strategic warhead has a yield of two megatons, the explosive equivalent of two million tons of TNT. But two million tons of TNT is about the same as all the bombs exploded in World War II—

a single bomb with the explosive power of the entire Second World War.

Carl Sagan • (1934–1996),
American astronomer

Following a nuclear attack on the United States, the U.S. Postal Service plans to distribute Emergency Change of Address Cards.

U.S. Federal Emergency Management
Agency (FEMA)

I refuse to accept the cynical notion that nation after nation must spiral down a militaristic stairway into the hell of nuclear destruction. I believe that unarmed truth and unconditional love will have the final word in reality.

Martin Luther King Jr.
(1929–1968), American
civil rights leader and
Nobel laureate

soldiers

IT IS ESSENTIAL TO PERSUADE THE SOLDIER THAT THOSE HE IS BEING URGED TO MASSACRE ARE BANDITS WHO DO NOT DESERVE TO LIVE; BEFORE KILLING OTHER GOOD, DECENT FELLOWS LIKE HIMSELF, HIS GUN WOULD FALL FROM HIS HANDS.

André Gide
(1869–1951), French author and Nobel laureate

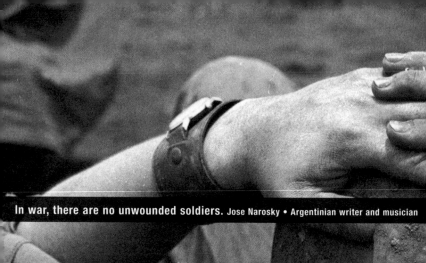

In war, there are no unwounded soldiers. Jose Narosky • Argentinian writer and musician

The time not to become a father is eighteen years before a war.

E. B. White • (1899–1985), American author

The soldier, above all other people, prays for peace, for he must suffer and bear the deepest wounds and scars of war.

Douglas MacArthur • (1880–1964), American army general

soldiers

Until the dead are buried, they change somewhat in appearance each day. The color change in Caucasian races is from white to yellow, to yellow-green, to black. If left long enough in the heat the flesh comes to resemble coal-tar, especially where it has been broken or torn, and it has quite a visible tarlike iridescence. The dead grow larger each day until sometimes they become quite too big for their uniforms, filling these until they seem blown tight enough to burst.

Ernest Hemingway
(1899–1961), American writer and Nobel laureate

Many a noble pair of steeds drew an empty chariot along the highways of war, for lack of drivers who were lying on the plain, more useful now to vultures than to their wives.

Homer
(ca. 700 BC), Greek poet

How senseless is everything that can ever be written, done, or thought, when such things are possible. It must be all lies and of no account when the culture of a thousand years could not prevent this stream of blood being poured out, these torture-chambers in their hundreds of thousands. A hospital alone shows what war is.

Erich Maria Remarque
(1898–1970), German author

War is always attractive to young men
who know nothing about it.

Philip Caputo
(1941–), American author and journalist

I hate war as only a soldier who has lived
it can, only as one who has seen its brutality,
its futility, and its stupidity.

Dwight D. Eisenhower
(1890–1969), American president

The blood of the soldier makes
the glory of the general.

Henry G. Bohn
(1796–1884), British publisher

The mass of men serves the state thus,
not as men mainly, but as machines, with
their bodies. They are the standing army,
and the militia, jailors, constables, posse
comitatus, etc. In most cases there is no
free exercise whatever of the judgment or
of the moral sense; but they put themselves
on a level with wood and earth and
stones; and wooden men can perhaps be
manufactured that will serve the purpose
as well. Such command no more respect
than men of straw or a lump of dirt.

Henry David Thoreau
(1817–1862), American author and philosopher

WHERE IS IT WRITTEN IN THE CONSTITUTION, IN WHAT ARTICLE OR SECTION IS IT CONTAINED, THAT YOU MAY TAKE CHILDREN FROM THEIR PARENTS, AND PARENTS FROM THEIR CHILDREN, AND COMPEL THEM TO FIGHT THE BATTLES OF ANY WAR IN WHICH THE FOLLY OR THE WICKEDNESS OF GOVERNMENT MAY ENGAGE IT?

Daniel Webster
(1782–1852), American statesman and lawyer

revenge

ALL THEY THAT TAKE THE SWORD SHALL PERISH WITH THE SWORD.

Matthew 26:52,
King James Version
of the Bible

Along the way of life, someone must have sense enough and morality enough to cut off the chain of hate. This can only be done by projecting the ethic of love to the center of our lives.

Martin Luther King Jr.
(1929–1968), American civil rights leader and Nobel laureate

We ought not to retaliate or render evil for evil to anyone, whatever evil we may have suffered from him.

Plato
(427–347 BC), Greek philosopher

You have heard that they were told, "An eye for an eye, a tooth for a tooth." But what I tell you is this: Do not resist those who wrong you. If anyone slaps you on the right cheek, turn and offer him the other also.

Matthew 5:38–39, revised English edition of the Bible

The use of force alone is but temporary. It does not remove the necessity of subduing again: and a nation is not governed, which is perpetually to be conquered.

Edmund Burke
(1729–1797), Irish statesman and political theorist

WHEN WE SEE A BLOW STRUCK, WE GO ON AND THINK NO MORE ABOUT IT: YET EVERY BLOW AIMED AT THE MOST DISTANT OF OUR FELLOW CREATURES IS SURE TO COME BACK, SOME TIME OR OTHER, TO OUR FAMILIES AND DESCENDANTS.

Walter Savage Landor
(1775–1864), English writer and poet

WHAT YOU DO NOT WANT DONE TO YOURSELF, DO NOT DO TO OTHERS.

Confucius
(551–479 BC), Chinese philosopher

IF ANYONE SHOULD GIVE YOU A BLOW WITH HIS HAND, WITH A STICK, OR WITH A KNIFE, YOU SHOULD ABANDON ANY DESIRES AND UTTER NO EVIL WORDS.

Buddha
(Siddhartha Gautama; ca. 563–483 BC), Indian spiritual teacher

war is not

"Skull"   BRANDON

the answer

hatred

HATRED IS THE
COWARD'S REVENGE FOR
BEING INTIMIDATED.

George Bernard Shaw
(1856–1950), Irish dramatist and political activist

✿

TRANSFORMING HATRED
OF AN ENEMY INTO COMPASSION
IS WHAT LIES AT THE SPIRITUAL
CORE OF ALL RELIGIONS.

Sister Helen Prejean
(1939–), Catholic nun

ONE WHO DOES NOT HATE ANY CREATURE, WHO IS FRIENDLY AND COMPASSIONATE . . . IS DEAR TO ME.

Bhagavad Gita, chapters 12:13, 12:14

The price of hating other human beings
is loving oneself less.

Eldridge Cleaver
(1935–1998), American author and civil rights leader

He who hates a man is as if he hated God.

Midrash

We have just enough religion to make us hate,
but not enough to make us love one another.

Jonathan Swift
(1667–1745), Irish writer and satirist

children

WAR LOVES TO SEEK ITS
VICTIMS IN THE YOUNG.

Sophocles
(ca. 495–406 BC), Greek playwright

IN PEACE, CHILDREN INTER
THEIR PARENTS; WAR VIOLATES
THE ORDER OF NATURE
AND CAUSES PARENTS TO INTER
THEIR CHILDREN.

Herodotus
(ca. 484–425 BC), Greek historian

WHAT ABOUT ME?

LABOUR for PEACE

No. 3.   PRINTED BY VICTORIA HOUSE PRINTING COMPANY LTD. (T.U.), DRURY LANE, W.C.2. PUBLISHED BY THE LABOUR PARTY, TRANSPORT HOUSE, SMITH SQUARE, LONDON, S.W.1.

WHEN ELEPHANTS FIGHT,

IT IS THE

GRASS

THAT

SUFFERS

African • (Kikuyu) proverb

I don't want to kill innocent mothers and children and fathers in another country when there are alternate means available. . . . And if any newscaster wanted to speak to any member of the PTA across America, I have a feeling they would say the same thing.

Rosie O'Donnell
(1962–), American talk-show host

I don't believe in harming people. I don't believe in bombing children. I don't believe in making misery when it's totally unnecessary. And misery is not necessary.

Alice Walker
(1944–), African American author

我們熱愛和平

I can still see the butchered women and children lying heaped and scattered all along the crooked gulch as plain as when I saw them with eyes still young. And I can see that something else died there in the bloody mud and was buried in the blizzard. A people's dream died there.

Black Elk
(1863–1950), Native American medicine man

Small boys are delirious with pride and joy as they fancy themselves thrusting swords into soft flesh and burning and laying waste such homes as they themselves inhabit.

Ernest Crosby
(1856–1907), American reformer and author

women

Wherever I go in the world as a professional peacemaker, I always find more women ready to take on the work of peace than men. Maybe it's because women and their children account for 80 percent of the casualties of today's wars.

Louise Diamond
American teacher and activist

Women have a place to fill and a stake to claim and a role to play in the world's pursuit of peace. Indeed, women have a right to judge the strategies that are becoming the instruments of war, and to suggest—no, to demand—the feminine alternatives of listening and seeing and caring and relating and reaching out and feeling for the other, that lead the world away from war.

Sister Joan D. Chittister
(1936–), Benedictine nun

Arise, then, women of this day! Arise all women who have hearts, whether our baptism be that of water or of tears! We will not have great questions decided by irrelevant agencies. Our sons shall not be taken from us to unlearn all that we have been able to teach them of charity, mercy, and patience.

Julia Ward Howe

(1819–1910), American poet and philanthropist

Mother's Day really was in its origin an anti-war day, and anti-war statement. Julia Ward Howe was sickened by what had happened during the Civil War; the loss of life, the carnage; and she created Mother's Day as a call for women all over the world to come together and create ways of protesting war, of making a kind of alternate government that could finally do away with war as an acceptable way of solving conflict.

Gloria Steinem

(1934–), American feminist, author, and peace activist

WOMEN OF BRITAIN

COME INTO
THE FACTORIES

ASK AT ANY EMPLOYMENT EXCHANGE FOR ADVICE AND FULL DETAILS

AS FAR AS WE ARE CONCERNED, EVERY SINGLE DEATH . . . IN EVERY WAR THAT WAS EVER FOUGHT REPRESENTS LIFE NEEDLESSLY WASTED, A MOTHER'S LABOR SPURNED. WE ARE FOR LIFE AND CREATION, AND WE ARE AGAINST WAR AND DESTRUCTION.

Betty Williams
(1943–), Irish Nobel laureate

AS A MOTHER,
I JUST WANT TO SEE
EVERY POSSIBLE
ALTERNATIVE EXHAUSTED

BEFORE
CHILDREN AND AMERICAN SOLDIERS'

LIVES ARE LOST.
I LOVE MY COUNTRY. I AM A
PROUD AMERICAN.

Natalie Maines
(1974–), American singer-songwriter

brother-
hood

A MYSTIC BOND OF BROTHERHOOD MAKES ALL MEN ONE.

Thomas Carlyle
(1795–1881), Scottish essayist, satirist, and historian

ALL MEN TREMBLE AT PUNISHMENT, ALL MEN FEAR DEATH: 'REMEMBER THAT YOU ARE LIKE UNTO THEM, AND DO NOT KILL NOR CAUSE SLAUGHTER.

Buddha
(Siddhartha Gautama; ca. 563–483 BC), Indian spiritual teacher

BE KINDLY AFFECTIONED ONE TO ANOTHER WITH BROTHERLY LOVE.

Paul 12:10, King James Version of the Bible

Any man's death diminishes me, because I am involved in Mankind. And therefore never send to know for whom the bell tolls; it tolls for thee.

John Donne
(1572–1631), English poet and preacher

If the basic human nature was aggressive, we would have been born with animal claws and huge teeth—but ours are very short, very pretty, very weak! That means we are not well equipped to be aggressive beings.

Tenzin Gyatso
(1935–), fourteenth Dalai Lama

The problem [of war] is a world problem. No nation can find its own salvation by breaking away from others. We must all be saved or we must all perish together.

Mahatma Gandhi
(1869–1948), Indian spiritual and political leader

We can choose

either to walk

the high road

of human

brother-
hood

or

the
low road
of man's
inhumanity
to man.

Martin Luther King Jr.
(1929–1968), American civil righ
leader and Nobel laureate

brotherhood

Man's
inhumanity

to man

makes

countless

thousands mourn.

Robert Burn
(1759–1796),
Scottish poet

141

peace

An ounce of peace is worth more
than a pound of victory.

Robert Bellarmine
(1542–1621), Roman Catholic cardinal and saint

God and the politicians willing,
the United States can declare peace
upon the world, and win it.

Ely Culbertson
(1891–1955), American author and activist

It isn't enough to talk about
peace. One must believe it. And it
isn't enough to believe in it. One
must work at it.

Eleanor Roosevelt
(1884–1962), American first lady and political activist

I think that people want peace so much that one of these days governments had better get out of the way and let them have it.

Dwight D. Eisenhower • (1890–1969), American president

I AM NOT ONLY A PACIFIST BUT A MILITANT PACIFIST. I AM WILLING TO **FIGHT** **FOR PEACE.** NOTHING WILL END WAR UNLESS THE PEOPLE REFUSE TO GO TO WAR

Albert Einstein • (1879–1955), German-born physicist and Nobel laureate

I'M NOT A PACIFIST.
I'M NOT THAT BRAVE.

Phil Donahue
(1935–), American talk-show host

PAX SO

VIETICA

The world will never have lasting peace
so long as men reserve for war the finest
human qualities. Peace, no less than war,
requires idealism and self-sacrifice and
a righteous and dynamic faith.

John Foster Dulles
(1888–1959), American secretary of state

The manhood that has been in war
must be transferred to the cause of peace,
before war can lose its charm, and
peace be venerable to men.

Ralph Waldo Emerson
(1803–1882), American essayist and poet

Peace hath her victories. No less renowned than war.

John Milton

(1608–1674), English poet

I see the world gradually being turned into a wilderness, I hear the ever approaching thunder, which will destroy us too. I can feel the sufferings of millions and yet, if I look up into the heavens, I think that it will all come right, that this cruelty too will end, and that peace and tranquility will return again.

Anne Frank

(1929–1945), German-born Jewish diarist

Peace is a daily, a weekly, a monthly process, gradually changing opinions, slowly eroding old barriers, quietly building new structures.

John F. Kennedy

(1917–1963), American president

THERE IS NO WAY TO PEACE. PEACE IS THE WAY.

A. J. Muste
(1885–1967), American activist

Perhaps the great day will come when a people, distinguished by wars and victories and by the highest development of a military order and intelligence, and accustomed to make the heaviest sacrifice for these things, will exclaim of its own free will, "we break the sword," and will smash its military establishment down to its lowest foundations.

Friedrich Nietzsche
(1844–1900), German philosopher

Let us not accept violence as the way of peace. Let us instead begin by respecting true freedom: The resulting peace will be able to satisfy the world's expectations, for it will be a peace built on justice, a peace founded on the incomparable dignity of the free human being.

John Paul II
(1920–2005), Catholic pope

PEACE HATH HIGHER
TESTS OF MANHOOD THAN
BATTLE EVER KNEW.

John Greenleaf Whittier
(1807–1892), American poet and abolitionist

OUR GOAL MUST NOT BE PEACE IN OUR TIME BUT PEACE FOR ALL TIME.

Harry S. Truman
(1884–1972), American president

Observe good faith and justice toward all nations.
Cultivate peace and harmony with all.

George Washington
(1732–1799), American president

Peace is the absence of war, but beyond that,
peace is a commodity unlike any other. Peace is
security. Peace is a mindset. Peace is a way of
living. Peace is the capacity to transcend past
hurts—to break cycles of violence and forge new
pathways that say, "I would like to make sure we
live as a community where there is justice, security,
and development for all members." At the end of
the day, peace is an investment; it is something
you create, by investing in a way of life.

Noeleen Heyzer
(1948–) Singaporean executive director of the United
Nations Development Fund for Women (UNIFEM)

★

There is a certain kind of peace that is not merely
the absence of war. It is larger than that. The peace
I am thinking of is not at the mercy of history's rule,
nor is it a passive surrender to the status quo. The
peace I am thinking of is the dance of an open mind
when it engages another equally open one.

Toni Morrison
(1931–) African American author and Nobel laureate

peace

All works of love are works of peace.

Mother Teresa • (1910–1997), Catholic nun,
missionary worker, and Nobel laureate

Nonviolence is a power which can be wielded
equally by all—children, young men and women
or grown-up people—provided they have a living
faith in the God of Love and have, therefore,
equal love for all mankind.

Mahatma Gandhi
(1869–1948), Indian spiritual and political leader

Nonviolence is the answer to the crucial political
and moral questions of our time; the need for man
to overcome oppression and violence without
resorting to oppression and violence. Mankind
must evolve for all human conflict a method which
rejects revenge, aggression, and retaliation.
The foundation of such a method is love.

Martin Luther King Jr.
(1929–1968), American civil rights leader and Nobel laureate

Nonviolence is not inaction. It is
not discussion. It is not for the timid or weak. . . .
Nonviolence is hard work.

Cesar Chavez
(1927–1993), Mexican American labor leader and civil rights activist

If we have no peace, it is because we have
forgotten that we belong to each other.

Mother Teresa
(1910–1997), Catholic nun, missionary worker, and Nobel laureate

We will have to want peace, want it enough to pay
for it, pay for it in our own behavior and in material
ways. We will have to want it enough to overcome
our lethargy and go out and find all those in other
countries who want it as much as we do.

Eleanor Roosevelt
(1884–1962), American first lady and political activist

Peace can start with just one heart.

Holly Near
(1949–), American teacher and songwriter

God loves us, understands our struggles,
and calls us to love ourselves for who we are—
imperfect but precious instruments of peace.

Catherine Whitmire
American chaplain, lecturer, and author

So we must remain steadfast in our knowledge
that . . . we are right, and we must remain hopeful
that for our children and our children's children, that
we are not a warring nation, but we will embrace and
practice true compassion and honor the ideals of
peace and freedom, and we will not give up. Peace.

Jessica Lange
(1942–), actress and peace activist

The real and lasting victories are
those of peace and not of war.

Ralph Waldo Emerson
(1803–1882), American essayist and poet

love

SOFT IS STRONGER THAN HARD, WATER THAN ROCK, LOVE THAN VIOLENCE.

Hermann Hesse

(1877–1962), German-born novelist, poet, and painter

Thou shalt love thy neighbor as thyself.

**Leviticus 19:18, King James
Version of the Bible**

A new commandment I give unto you, that ye
love one another. Just as a mother would protect
her only child at the risk of her own life, even so,
cultivate a boundless heart towards all beings.

Buddha
(Siddhartha Gautama; ca. 563–483 BC), Indian spiritual teacher

Love rules his kingdom without a sword.

George Herbert
(1593–1633), Welsh poet and priest

Do not waste time bothering whether you
"love" your neighbor; act as if you did. As soon
as we do this we find one of the great secrets.
When you are behaving as if you loved someone,
you will presently come to love him.

C. S. Lewis
(1898–1963), Irish author and scholar

No one is born hating another person
because of the color of his skin, or his
background, or his religion. People must
learn to hate, and if they can learn to hate,
they can be taught to love, for love
comes more naturally to the human
heart than its opposite.

Nelson Mandela
(1918–), South African president and Nobel laureate

YOU WILL NOT ENTER PARADISE UNTIL YOU HAVE FAITH, AND YOU WILL NOT COMPLETE YOUR FAITH UNTIL YOU LOVE ONE ANOTHER.

Muhammad
(ca. 570–632), Prophet of Islam

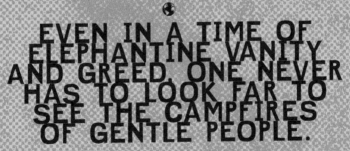

EVEN IN A TIME OF ELEPHANTINE VANITY AND GREED, ONE NEVER HAS TO LOOK FAR TO SEE THE CAMPFIRES OF GENTLE PEOPLE.

Garrison Keillor
(1942–), American author and humorist

activism

HELL NO, WE WON'T GO!

Anonymous American draft-resistance slogan (ca. 1970)

It had to take a war for people to learn that things could be defied and resisted. I think that was a very important legacy of the peace movement.

Grace Paley
(1922–2007), American author and peace activist

I don't want to put any more of our children in the hands of the warmongers and the war machine and the war profiteers. I think that would be a terrible idea. If there is a draft, I would just tell everybody with draft-age children, and draft-age children, to resist, resist, resist.

Cindy Sheehan
(1957–), American anti-war activist

Wars are not "acts of God." They are caused by man, by man-made institutions, by the way in which man has organized his society. What man has made, man can change.

Frederick Moore Vinson
(1890–1953), American Supreme Court justice

The voice of protest, of warning, of appeal is never more needed than when the clamor of fife and drum, echoed by the press and too often by the pulpit, is bidding all men fall in and keep step and obey in silence the tyrannous word of command.

Then, more than ever, it is the duty of the good citizen not to be silent.

Charles Eliot Norton • (1827–1908), American scholar

Activism is my rent for living on this planet.

Alice Walker

(1944–), African American writer

The question is not, "Can you make a difference?"
You already do make a difference. It's just a
matter of what kind of difference you want to
make during your life on this planet.

Julia Butterfly Hill

(1974–), American activist

Never doubt that a small number of dedicated
people can change the world; indeed, it is the
only thing that ever has.

Margaret Mead

(1901–1978), American cultural anthropologist

You may be disappointed if you fail,
but you are doomed if you don't try.

Beverly Sills

(1929–), American opera singer

IT IS NEVER TOO LATE TO DO RIGHT.

Ralph Waldo Emerson

(1803–1882), American essayist and poet